Jude Watts

A[

My Sh(
From Argl

A Journey from Confusion and Frustration
to Revelation and Calm

To my three Gorgeous Boys,

Thank you for making me the Proudest Mum.

Love you

ACKNOWLEDGEMENTS

Thank you to:

My loyal dog who sat by my feet for hours as I wrote, occasionally jumping up for affection and to look me in the eyes and plead, surely, it's break time now!

My coaching colleagues who have always been so encouraging and supportive.

My daughter-in-law (ish) for her creative talents and fun design discussions.

My best friend for well, simply being himself and being my best friend for oh so many years.

My love, for his endless, unconditional love and for always managing to make me laugh.

And finally for my darling sons who make our family time, loud, chaotic and wonderful.

ADHD

Would you like to know what this ADHD thing is all about?

Some people are sceptical it even exists, others are bemused by the sudden growth in its diagnosis, comments from the uninformed suggest it didn't exist years ago through to it's just an excuse for bad behaviour, bad parenting or even laziness.

I write from the viewpoint of someone who had no idea I even needed to know about it, to living with it as a parent daily and have life take me on a journey of discovery, being an advocate for my son and even becoming a coach and NLP Practitioner (Neuro Linguistic Programming). This book is designed to be easy to read and simple to understand, sharing my experiences and approaches, to give you a clear, enlightening perspective on ADHD. Taking the angst out of difficult moments and encouraging the heartfelt delight of the wonderous moments.

Primarily intended for parents, partners, and loved ones of individuals with ADHD, offering valuable insights to help them better understand and support those they care about. While especially beneficial for loved ones, it may also be helpful for anyone with an ADHD diagnosis, those awaiting one, or those who suspect they may have ADHD. Additionally, it provides useful guidance for colleagues and managers working alongside individuals with ADHD.

Throughout this book, alongside referring to my son, I will say they or them, by this I mean, those with ADHD. I do acknowledge some like to say are ADHD or ADHDers meaning they don't like the thought they 'have' ADHD but that they 'are' ADHD. This is an ever-changing landscape with many different attitudes towards this, some do want to be defined by it, others don't.
For the purposes of my book, I know my son and I are happy with saying he has ADHD, by the way just in case you are wondering I don't have ADHD, I write as an observer.

INTRODUCTION

ADHD stands for Attention Deficit Hyperactivity Disorder. I can easily see where the name came from, it has tried to describe what it looks like, perhaps trying to be helpful rather than just a naming after a doctor who discovered it which gives us no clue to what it actually is.

In terms of ADHD, attention deficit means easily distracted and hyperactivity means a need to constantly move, but to some degree, in trying to sum it up in a couple of words, it does it an injustice, in my opinion. Calling it a disorder immediately makes everyone feel something is wrong – is that really the case? Isn't it just that they are different, not better or worse?

One thing that is true, and they certainly agree, is that they don't have much order in their lives. This is a struggle for them because of differences in their executive functioning. Saying there is an attention deficit isn't strictly true, they have plenty of attention to give, under the right conditions for them. Alternative names that don't include negative connotations could be 'interest-based attention personality' or 'creative-thinking risk takers' or 'active minds and bodies type', the list is endless if you attempt to combine some of the traits, I have often thought about what would be the best name and come up with a few…but ultimately, I think it doesn't matter what title it has, it's about us all understanding it.

I also find it a little awkward that it is categorised as a disability, in legal terms, for places of work to ensure employers take responsibility for any adjustments needed. That in itself would appear to be a particularly divisive situation for those with ADHD and those without. Some like the acknowledgement and power it gives them to demand extra support, some resent being seen as having a disability and then choose not to disclose in order to not distinguish themselves from others and be seen as 'normal'.

The same goes for schools, they categorise a person with ADHD as having Special Educational Needs (SEN) in order for the child to get extra support and for example, extra time in exams. This is met with a mixed response from both children and parents, some grateful for the recognition and support, some unhappy to be put into such a broad category that they don't recognise the need for themselves to be included in, for example, some SEN have a significant learning delay and won't be expected to obtain any formal qualifications whilst someone with ADHD may well be very advanced academically.

One thing is for sure, everyone is an individual and this book will just give you a brief overview of some of the commonalities, as with everything - it will not apply to all.

QUOTE - ANONYMOUS

Your secrets are safe with me, because there's a good chance I was not listening.

WHAT ADHD IS AND WHAT IT IS NOT

Some descriptions taken from NHS website:

- Attention Deficit Hyperactivity Disorder is a condition that affects people's behaviour. People with ADHD can seem restless, may have trouble concentrating and may act on impulse.
- It can often be treated with medicines and talking therapies.
- It's not clear what causes ADHD but it tends to run in families.
- There are two categories of ADHD Inattentiveness and Hyperactivity & Impulsiveness, you can be diagnosed with Combined, this is the most common diagnosis.

Long misunderstood, it is not:
- Just being naughty
- Just boys
- Just children

Approximate statistics that are currently being quoted online by a variety of organisations:

- 5% of children in the UK have been diagnosed with ADHD
- 3-4% of adults in the UK have been diagnosed with ADHD – many adults are being diagnosed at the same time as their children.
- Girls have been less diagnosed because they often have the Inattentive Type, whereby they are quietly distracted, which

can go unnoticed, but the expectation is diagnosis will be equal between male and female.

- Breakdown of diagnosis
    - Combined – 50-75%
    - Hyperactive & Impulsive – 15%
    - Inattentive – 20-30%
- Those with ADHD have up to a 30% delay in Executive Functioning – this includes memory, planning, organisation, time management and focus
- 5% of people have ADHD
- 40% of those who have ADHD have Dyslexia

MY JOURNEY AND EXPERIENCES

My first connection with ADHD was over 16 years ago with my youngest son, he displayed characteristics that were so different to what I had seen before, that I started to have questions. That's when I started my research, I talked to family, friends and professionals, I read information from all over the place. This book will take you through the journey that I have experienced pre and post his diagnosis, my becoming aware and understanding ADHD and helping order the disorder!

0-5 years old

The very first thing I remember that started my questioning, was at the age of 6 months he attempted to climb out of his high chair! At this point in his life, I think he could barely sit unsupported and not crawl but he managed to get himself out, fortunately he did not fall but whilst catching him and holding him afterwards, I thought oh wow we have a live wire here, I can't rest on my laurels. I knew from his brothers that boys are active, but this was, well this simply, was different. From that day forth I have had to give an extra level of attention.

Fast forward to 18 months old, he managed to climb out of his cot, so up over the sides and down the other side to the floor. This I was prepared for (he was not the first to do this, his eldest brother also had), I had a rolled-up duvet lying next to the cot to soften the landing. To prevent any accidents going forward, knowing he now would climb out again thrilled by his new skill, he began to sleep in a bed with a rolled-up duvet on the floor just in case but to my knowledge, he never ever fell out.

It was also at this time, when he was 18 months old, that he was first exposed to a trampoline. I am sure it sounds young but we bought one for his middle brother's birthday and like I always do, I researched getting one and was advised by an official trampoline producer that the best way to learn to trampoline safely is not with a net but with a low trampoline and proper monitoring and guidance. Children don't learn to protect themselves when they are being protected. His brother would bounce on it continuously and, I could see him looking longingly. One day, I said I wonder...and let him try. He absolutely loved it and he was amazing. The advice was spot on and I am so grateful for it, all 3 of my sons enjoyed the freedom and not once fell off and injured themselves, it allowed them to have a fun activity whilst learning techniques and becoming responsible – is still can hear all our laughter and see my awe as they did their spectacular jumps.

The first impulsivity action I saw was when he was 2 years old, the TV was on, I can only assume he wanted something else on rather than what was on, as he went to the remote control on the table and obviously unable to work the remote properly by himself, he threw is at the TV, yes as you can imagine the TV screen cracked! It all happened so fast, we were all in shock and he couldn't really explain what had just happened and why. I had flashbacks to the climbing out of his highchair moment and again thought my word, he is really going to test my parenting skills!

Another time when he was still 2 years old, I was in a shop changing room trying on some jeans with him in there with me, when he announced he needed to go to the toilet, argh I thought great timing as I am stood with no trousers on. Ok I say, one second let me get dressed, unable to wait as I turn to get my clothes he crawls out under the door, arghh. I had to open the door, call him, and at the same time, cover myself, then put on my trousers whilst running after him, catching him and running back to collect bags etc from the changing room. Finally, we left the shop, found a toilet and returned to the shop and start all over again.

I think he was around 3 or 4 years old one bonfire night when he literally went missing. I was standing with the boys and my friend and her children, we all were looking up at the fireworks, my sons by my side...or so I thought. Clearly, as it turns out, he was not that impressed by the fireworks. Something must have distracted my youngest, the best way for me to describe these types of moments is

'Squirrel'. Like when a dog may well be running around happily and then sees a squirrel, whatever they were doing has been completely overridden by the need to chase the squirrel. As soon as I noticed, which can only have been a matter of a few minutes since I last saw and was speaking to him, we searched everywhere, calling, asking around. It was a big event and they had lots of marshals and emergency services there on standby. I informed a marshal and then, well, I was mortified by the trouble that then caused. They decided they had to lock down the place, no one could enter or leave until he was found. They asked us to go to the area where the emergency services vehicles were gathered, on arriving there, who do we see at the front of a fire engine being entertained by a fire fighter? Oh yes, my youngest, without a care in the world. Just pleasantly surprised to see us there assuming probably that we too found the fire engine way more interesting than the fireworks. He was completely oblivious to the chaos and worry he had caused and wasn't the slightest bit worried that he was lost. Later he just says, very confidently, I knew you'd find me, it didn't occur to him to feel at all scared, this was one big adventure. I remember feeling proud that he had the confidence that I would always be there to catch him, so to speak, but at the same time I was scared that he didn't experience fear like I would have expected, like we all need to have to protect ourselves.

5-10 years old

He continued to be an active person, being great at any physical activity asked of him. One time, I remember him being asked to do a long jump on sports day at primary school, but he wasn't that keen to it because it didn't look that interesting to him. This is of fundamental importance, he needs something to be interesting to him, for him to be interested in it. He was encouraged to do it and went from never having taken a long jump before, to being the best in his year that very day after that one jump. This moment encapsulates ADHD, their abilities are infinite (and why they are sometimes referred to, divisively, as having superpowers) but not always known as it takes a certain set of conditions for them to want to do something.

This had always been the case right from his first school, he had joined gymnastics and karate clubs and taken them to the highest level the school offered, which was for Year 2, he was in Reception Year at the time. I had to find a Karate club elsewhere and take him there after school. He continued to trampoline and became very good but never wanted to join a club. Even at a young age, he couldn't commit to things, he would grow tired of things and get bored and then there was no chance of him going to them. I took him to try many different sports and activities, football, rugby, athletics, ice skating, roller skating to name but a few but also learning French and Spanish to see if he enjoyed languages, he didn't! One sport that has remained to this day is climbing and bouldering. I think it's the combination of using his mind to work out the routes and the physical challenge that keeps this as a stimulating activity for him. It is also something you can do alone when you want to or with friends.

He was a fast runner and was good on the wing at rugby but got bored of waiting for the ball, we joined an athletics club when he was around 7 years old, he enjoyed the running and racing but again, not the waiting around for his race. When in London we joined a big athletics club and he ran at a large stadium and for the first time we were faced with a different problem and it was a new response from him that I had to digest. When things came naturally and easy to him, he took it for granted and could take or leave the situation. When things were a challenge, that was perfect, but there is a very small window for the sweet spot because if he is challenged with something that he believes is beyond his reach, he deems it pointless. Why strive for something you can never achieve, that is always going to leave you with the feeling of disappointment. This is my first time seeing Rejection Sensitive Dysphoria (RSD) in earnest, even if it is just a perception and does not turn out to be the reality, switching off and not engaging and missing the opportunity is better than trying and not succeeding in his opinion and nothing would sway him.

He was maybe 6/7 years old when we all were at a Pantomime, I know they encourage audience participation but he called out at a moment that definitely was not a moment for that, the theatre was silent at this point, the exact words I now can't remember but started with "Lady you don't want to do that", I would like to point out that this was the 'Principal Boy' character he was addressing who in pantomime is played by a woman. It sounds a funny moment, and now we can laugh but at the time it definitely was not and his brothers looked so embarrassed. He had a need to help her/him and couldn't stop himself calling out and saw no wrong in doing so.

When he was around 8 years old, we went on a family trip to New York, all of us walking down a street, he decides he likes something in a shop window and walks in, not saying a word to anyone, we are all in conversation and I look to say something to him and he's not there. Very quickly he is found in the shop next to where we are on the street but it could have been so much worse had him not being with us, not been noticed so quickly. He had absolutely no regard for the situation, other's concern or for his own safety. He was so shocked to find us cross with him.

When we had a puppy, I specifically asked everyone to keep the kitchen door shut, so he couldn't get out. He definitely knew and understood but multiple times he left the door open, there is something about not being able to keep all necessary information in the forefront of his mind. It's in there but at any moment can be overlooked. One time the puppy went upstairs and wet my bed. I was so cross I shouted and now that moment became memorable to him, a stronger connection maybe in his mind, because it then didn't happen again.

10-15 years old

Over the years I can't even count the number of things he has spilt, broken or lost. He has left jumpers, jackets, bags, iPods, phones, headphones and many more things in all manner of places cars, trains, planes, schools, restaurants, cinemas, theatres and of course at home when we are out and he needed them. In some rare cases, we have been able to retrieve but in most they are lost, never to be seen again. My words to him are now said on repeat daily – have you got…, did you remember…, check you have…

When we would go on any journey, from a day trip to a holiday abroad, I would find myself going through an invisible checklist with him multiple times, even when I reminded him to go to the toilet, he would forget. So, one of the first things we had to do was stop so he could go to the toilet, frustrating? oh yes! He also would always say he was not hungry when we had food to eat but a short while later, he would say I am hungry. All young children can be like this with going to the toilet and eating but he is the same to this day.

One day when he was only about 11 years old, walking home from school there was a stall selling these new hot potato snacks that everyone was buying, quite fancying one, full of confidence, charm and no fear, he asked the man next to him, "Can I borrow some money to buy one please, my mum will give it back to you", the man it turns out was impressed with his method of how he was trying to find a solution to his problem that he produced a £20 note and said "Buy one and keep the change young man" He has again had good fortune when on a rainy, a kindly shop keeper, who he always took the time to smile and say hello to every day as he passed, gave him an umbrella. His natural friendly, easy and kind character has proven to reward him and he has been given many food samples from market stalls. These experiences have had an amazing effect on him and he wants to 'pay it forward', he always wants to speak to and support anyone living on the streets.

Asking him to do something is quite a task in itself. You make the request at least about 10 times, for example, "Can you tidy your room please?", this is usually met with a simple "Yeah". By the 11th time, your request has turned into a firm demand, for example, "Tidy you room now!", oddly this is met with confusion and he is taken aback by the firmness. He will then make statements like why didn't you just ask. At this point, you don't know whether to laugh or cry, you check your sanity with internal thoughts of, 'have I entered a time warp' and so forth.

When he has misplaced things, he doesn't give the most obvious place a thorough search. He immediately jumps to the conclusion that things are lost/left behind somewhere because they're not exactly where he thought, as in the very exact place. One day, he returns home from climbing and after a quick check at home, he then tells me he must have left his phone there, quite confidently, he said it would be there as it wasn't in his jacket pocket or in his room. Whilst in the discussion of trying to work out why he thought that, when did he last have it etc., he leaves for the climbing centre calmly assuming it would be there, it wasn't. It was in his climbing bag, so whilst he went back to the climbing centre, I started to look through his bag, not the nicest of jobs if anyone knows what climbing shoes smell like, anyway, ta-da, there was his phone. Obviously, I can't contact him to tell him, so he returns home a lot more concerned now, to then be delighted to discover I found it in his bag. He then suddenly declares "Oh yeah, I remember now I did put it in my bag".

You'd possibly think that when only a week later a very similar situation happened but this time with his keys that he would give his climbing bag a thorough check, no he didn't, he again assumed he had left them at the climbing centre, I immediately checked his bag (armed with Febreeze this time) and low and behold, there they were. What I have observed is that he has no recollection of a mundane, automatic, sensible actions like putting something in his bag for safekeeping, and his go to, is to assume the worst. So, despite the fact that he has done the clever thing and stored it safely, he naturally jumps to the conclusion that he has done something silly and left or forgotten it. This I believe is another example of RSD.

One of the things that I have adapted to is the acceptance of, what I see as important and what I feel is important are not the same for my son. A daily routine used to include me being a nag, there is no other word for it. I can still hear myself saying can you open your curtains, in fact open the window and let some fresh air in. Pick up your wet towel, make your bed, put your dirty clothes in the wash basket, you get the scene. This, as you can imagine was frustrating and tiring. I thought it's fine, I went through this with his older brothers and eventually they learnt and adapted themselves (still not sure about the making the bed part though!). For my youngest, he, to this day, has not learnt or adapted. This most definitely is not about laziness or stubbornness, this is about not seeing it and not feeling its importance. One day I just stopped asking and overnight my stress and annoyance went. It's me who saw the mess, it's me that wanted the light and fresh air, so it was me who sorted it. It took me less than 2 minutes to open the curtains, open the window, hang up his wet towel, make his bed and put his dirty clothes in the wash basket. I am sure what I do will be met by some as wrong but it has made our life happier and calmer and I genuinely don't mind getting that for the 2 minutes of effort each day, life is about choices and that is what I choose over nagging any day. This isn't about educating my son any longer, it is way beyond that, this is about accepting he has ADHD and he experiences the world and life differently to me.

On the subject of cleaning, I am always amazed at the result, I seriously never know what I am going to get, see later how he empties the dishwasher. One time when I asked him to clean the bathroom, hours later the bathroom was still not quite clean but the extractor fan looked like new. You have to laugh but yes, he spent hours with a wooden cocktail stick cleaning the dust off the extractor fan.

16 years old and beyond...

When he turned 16 years old, I encouraged him, as I had done with his brothers and as I had done as a teenager, to look for a part-time job. This in my opinion, not only does the obvious and provide him with money for his hobbies and social activities but develops responsibility and the value of things and money.

He approached this with his ADHD ways and applied for hundreds of jobs, any jobs, literally anything. Could be full-time, could be senior management, again you had to laugh, and feel sorry for the companies that sent polite rejections. But his scatter gun approach worked and one day he got a call and was given a phone interview on the spot. He had absolutely no idea what job it was he was being interviewed for, he told me once off the call, all he knew was this was a preliminary chat to see if the manager should call for a longer phone interview.

Somehow, he passed that first call with his 'gift of the gab' and a manager would call later. All we knew was the location the job was at. Based on that information we had to go back online and find the job advert, of course he had not made a note of any of his applications.
We found it, phew, so knowing that a call was imminent, what did he do, wait and be available, no, he went climbing, telling me it would be fine, he would climb with his earphones. Ok I thought, that might work and possibly it could have done, had he not left his phone on the kitchen table. The end of the story is he got that job, despite missing the manager's first call, one thing my son is, is full of charm.

That particular job didn't last long as the manager decided to get rid of half the workforce and replace with family and did a 'last in, first out' approach.

On the back of his previous success, straight away he starts applying for a variety of roles again, a little bit more specific this time. The story this time goes that he gets a response to one job inviting him for an interview that he overlooks and picks up after the date of the interview. He instantly emails apologising and gets another interview. Afterwards despite me asking him to check his emails to see if he got the job, he doesn't check, assuming he didn't, he actually had, he decided to check after about a week and saw they wanted him to start the following week.

This to me is another occasion that connects to RSD. He would rather not deal with the rejection, so easier to just assume he didn't get it.

QUOTE - ANONYMOUS

At the age of 52 I went to my first ADHD Conference. People were spilling things, losing keys and getting lost!
I was home.

SCHOOLS

Pre-school

Based on what I had experienced with my son over his first few years, I chose a small, independent pre-school/nursery, walking distance from home. At this stage I decided I wanted him to not be in a big, busy and structured environment, but more of a nurturing, child-led place. This was a good decision and perfect for a while but I could see after some time the novelty for him had worn off and his creativity and imagination decreased. The freedom was great and he started off happy but now although not unhappy he had lost any enthusiasm. There were meetings and discussions with the pre-school and we worked together to help him. We all used to say the same, he was bright and funny and everyone loved him, teachers and other children but we could never quite get him to 'conform'. What I mean by that is he seemed to want to march to the beat of his own drum, as they say. Sometimes very involved in an activity and super engaged with all, another day quite the opposite. Chats to him about it, shed absolutely no light on the situation, he couldn't explain why.

Primary School – No. 1

For his primary school, I had a choice of two very different schools to send him to, one very similar in ethos to the pre-school (and the one his brothers went to) or one that was very structured and strict. This time, based on how he reacted after a while at his pre-school, I opted for the structured, strict one, hoping that this school would be able to keep on top of him and keep him motivated. Sadly, this did not work out at all as I hoped, he was getting more and more withdrawn, he was very regularly in trouble due to their strict rules and ultimately there were tears and requests to not go to school. The school in the meantime had got him to sit some tests, he and I were unaware of this but the results showed to them he fell into a 'gifted and talented' category, which to some degree explained a lot. Although it changed nothing, they gave him some harder work e.g. maths from the year above etc to keep him challenged and stimulated but their environment meant they still required him to adhere to rules and the standard sized class for a state school meant the teacher was unable to give him an extra attention and more so really didn't need him distracting others because he was starting to get very easily distracted himself.

Primary School – No. 2

I decided that I wanted to try a private school, I knew their class sizes were considerably smaller and I hoped the attention he might receive would really help with his concentration. I had seen that any one-to-one work either at home or school helped enormously with keeping his attention focused on what he was doing. As before with both the pre-school and his first primary school, that start was good. With the benefit of hindsight this is because it was a new environment, novel, so with him having ADHD (still undiagnosed at this point) he could focus as it was interesting, something new to discover and explore. At the same time the teachers found him new and interesting so the whole situation feels like it is working. What ends up happening and did again is after some time the teachers become exhausted and frustrated. In this particular school I had started down the route of speaking to doctors about him.

Primary School No. 3

I could tell that move to that school had not helped at all, what was I to do, all I wanted was my son in a happy, healthy environment that enabled him to learn. Again, this school had told me, he's bright, funny and widely liked. The situation was getting quite upsetting. I considered home schooling, I chatted to old teachers of my other sons' regarding tutoring, I was exploring all options. I finally went with a suggestion of a small, village school (state run). Like one big family every child would know every child in the school, all parents would know each other, this could work with my constant involvement. It did in the main, he was happy, tick. He was learning, tick. I was constantly involved with the school as different teachers handled him in different ways, in simple terms if someone was strict and relentless with their style, it failed spectacularly. If someone was gentle, kind and encouraging, he flourished. Of course, not everyone is that in life, so we had good days and bad.

Primary School No. 4

We moved house from the country to London with one more year of primary school to go. He was enrolled at the local school and again was happy and settled well. In fact, within the first few days, he was encouraged to do a long jump for the first time, as previously mentioned, but he wasn't as impressed as we all were, he shrugged, yeah but that was easy. He didn't seem to appreciate his natural talent. I spotted it hadn't excited or challenged him, things that were exciting or challenging, now that was different then we'd see him motivated. He was invited to do a speech in front of his class about a given topic, he did it so well I was contacted by the head teacher, not only was he articulate he came up with ideas that no-one had considered.

It was in this school in London for the last year of primary school that they reached out to me regarding him being referred to a doctor for assessment for possible ADHD – Halleluiah. I can't tell you how happy I was, that for 10 years I knew there was something but now someone else was acknowledging they saw it too.

Secondary School

Starting secondary school with the diagnosis I thought would help, surely, they would have understanding and support, well in a word no. It would appear that the system in place regarding diagnosis at the time was good in London but as for schools they just didn't have the understanding or provision required. Very quickly, I mean within weeks he was getting in to trouble for very minor things but they had many rules, more than I could read. Without going into too much detail the school inhibited his learning by giving him constant punishments, it was one of the most stressful periods of my life.

I have never been contacted so often for things that all boiled down to him having ADHD. I couldn't get them to stop crushing him. He got distressed, as did I and his teachers at the school. The only thing that got me through was sheer determination to always support my son no matter what. I pointed out their unfairness, their lack of knowledge, lack of required skills and always made my son feel I understood him and would not let this stop him being happy and achieving.

I so wished and still do wish that there would be an awareness and understanding of ADHD across all schools then a bigger acceptance will be made for those that are late, forget homework, get distracted in lessons, lose PE bags etc but also are full of ideas, creative, engaging, funny, happy, kind individuals. I would get reports and attend parent's evening to hear the same stories again and again. He's such a nice boy, well mannered, well behaved, interesting, interested but he gets distracted, often late, often not got the books or equipment he needs, often breaks rules including hugging friends (no touching allowed), going up/down wrong stairs, not having his planner out on his desk (a school rule). He would start to switch off not understanding why these things were so important.

To this day and probably always he will be late, he will lose things, he will forget things – it is part and parcel of having ADHD. Suffering twice because you are then punished for it whilst at school is a tough pill to swallow and helps no-one, least of all my son who they are trying to educate. I so wished they concentrated on educating him with skills and knowledge and stopped trying to make him better at the things that will never improve just because they said he must. Improvements in those areas take time, over a lifetime to come up with strategies and techniques to help.

Over the years I trained in coaching and ADHD and try whenever possible to spread awareness – one reason for writing this book.

WHAT ADHD LOOKS LIKE

- Careless mistakes
- Trouble holding attention
- Not appearing to listen
- Trouble organising tasks
- Often loses things
- Often easily distracted
- Often forgetful
- Often fidgets or taps
- Often gets up and walks around
- Often unable to be quiet
- Often on the go as if driven by a motor
- Trouble waiting their turn
- Often interrupts or intrudes on others
- Often talks excessively

ROAD TO DIAGNOSIS

Firstly, word of warning if you have to go down this road, be prepared to wait and wait and wait. You discuss everything with your GP, they refer you to child psychologists and paediatricians and all this takes a long time.

In the meantime, I was also offered a parenting course for parents with children that have challenging behaviour. On the surface it is a nice thing, they are trying to support you as they can tell life is quite difficult to parent this complicated situation without any understanding of what is going on. The reality is though that the course helps those that have badly behaved children for a variety of reasons and parents that lack the skills or energy to cope. This was not reflective of my situation at all. I worked hard to understand the differences my son experienced and he didn't behave badly. What he was displaying was classic traits of ADHD, easily distracted, trouble focussing, needed to be active often. The course did nothing to help me, my son or the situation.

Appointments with the paediatrician started to see if there was anything medically going on, there wasn't but she left me with an interesting and odd piece of advice, I recounted many stories of things that happened in our day to day lives, one being that at the supermarket he would run off, run up and down aisles and disappear. She said "Well, just let him then!" Flabbergasted, it was then I thought many people just don't get what it is like parenting a child that acts this way. Just let him, my word, I am sure her advice was coming from a good place to help me be less stressed and for my son to be able to just be himself but unfortunately life isn't like that. Losing your son and affecting others whilst trying to go about a daily task, is not fun to say the least.

Finally, we see a psychologist that suggests I complete a form alongside the school completing the same form. It asks a series of questions about how he is at home and school with regards to many aspects. You both independently complete them and return them, then based on the comparison and similarity to the responses it would get referred to a psychiatrist to make a diagnosis.

What a disaster that turned out to be. At this point in life, he is in a private school, the set up and ethos was very different to state schools. To begin with they had no SEN provision at all and did not have any Educational Psychologists, so they were unaware of these situations and lack any understanding of them. If I wanted or needed either of them, I would have to pay the cost of them. They also don't accept many SEN situations and don't want to 'label' a young child as that might hinder the child in their progress and life but they also don't want anything to affect their stable 'normal' school and 'good' results. They I believe, fear if they were known to have children with 'disabilities' that might stop some parents wanting to send their children there. Hopefully things have changed in this last decade but that was the reality then. So, they completed the form and no other way to explain it, they lied. Quite proudly lied, taking me to one side letting me know that they didn't want to disclose the true situation as they thought it would be unfair to label a young child and they didn't want to be the cause of him being diagnosed. His teacher was absolutely lovely, was very fond of my son and I had a good relationship with her but what she did was hold back his diagnosis for 4 years sadly, thinking she was helping him and I and most probably the school.

It was in his final year of primary school when we lived in London, that he received his diagnosis. The process this time seemed to be quite quick and efficient, after his school referred us to the GP, the GP referred us to the local CAMHS (Child and Adolescent Mental Health Services). We went through the process of both me and the school completing forms as well as a few visits in person with my son to CAMHS and seeing a psychiatrist who diagnosed him, the school this time had accurately completed the form with the truth of the situation.

HOW ADHD CAN AFFECT LIFE

- Poor sense of time
- All or nothing attitude
- Difficulty maintaining relationships
- Executive dysfunction
- Forgetting to eat, sleep or go to the toilet
- Inability to focus even if no distractions
- Depression
- Difficulty following conversations
- Trouble recalling words
- RSD (Rejection Sensitive Dysphoria)
- Sleeping problems
- Poor impulse control
- Mood swings
- Choice/Decision paralysis

MEDICATION

I will only briefly state anything about medication from our own situation. I will not give advice or advocate for or against it. At the beginning after the diagnosis, we continued as we had for his whole life, without medication but managing it with understanding and care. After a while his life a school became difficult, constantly getting into trouble for things that in the main were connected to his ADHD. We tried ADHD medication for a year or so, the situation at school did not improve enough for us to warrant continuing, one of the side effects are loss of appetite and at this prime growth time I didn't want that affected. I also had opted for a dose that started at 8am and wore off by 4pm and he didn't take it at the weekends. I liked the way he was naturally, as did he, we were only taking it for the benefit of the school but they still made his life hard by dishing out constant punishments.

REJECTION SENSITIVE DYSPHORIA (RSD)

Another odd, long title that really doesn't explain what it is very well, again I don't blame the title as this one is hugely complex and, in some respects, I would say dominates a lot of who a person with ADHD is, this affects their whole sense of being. I am not medically trained and I myself do not have ADHD, so, as with all the book I am only going to state what I have heard and observed and the conclusions I have drawn.

The simple definition is this is a term used to describe the intense emotions felt when exposed to real or perceived rejection, criticism or failure. Symptoms can include low self-esteem, self-doubt, negative self-talk, difficulty managing reactions and sudden outbursts of physical emotions like anger, tears and sadness.

As I have mentioned throughout the book this occurs many times for different situations and can cause difficulties. Having an understanding that it exists and being able to spot it happening will help with trying to overcome the problems it can cause.

POEM BY MHA

She was never
on the same page
as the people
around her.
Sometimes ahead
sometimes behind,
always in a different
chapter,
sometimes even
in a completely different
book.

CHARACTERISTICS OF ADHD

When pondering on how best to describe the states of being that I have observed I found myself saying – the Interrupter, the Fidgeter, the Dreamer. I then decided to use some the titles from Roger Hargreaves' Mr Men and Little Miss books alongside some of my own I made up. I will leave them as Mr and Little Miss but of course this applies to all.

The Interrupter

You can imagine the scene, people mid-conversation and up they bounce, excitedly they blurt out whatever it is on their mind.

First impressions could be they see themselves as more important or they see their information as important or urgent. People's responses vary from, ignoring and carrying own conversation till that is concluded then turning to let them speak, right through to stopping talking and allowing the interruption, expecting to hear something that needed to be shared right away. The patient ones that allowed the interruption will probably be dismayed as they hear just some information, neither important or urgent on their scale. Those that turned to hear the information after finishing their conversation will be confused to find the person with ADHD no longer is there or no longer can remember what it was, they wanted to say.

The person with ADHD does not see themselves or the information as more important but and here is the thing, they have to say it right away or they will forget it, it's as simple as that.

Their urgency to let you know comes from their experience of when they have waited, they lose the thought, completely lose it, very often for it to never return.

My approach: I have learned to let the interruptions happen generally and thank and explain afterwards to the person I was speaking to.

The Fidgeter

This comes in all the forms you can imagine, from fiddling with things, anything, switches, buttons, things lying on a table in front of them to tapping or jiggling legs as well as not being able to sit in one place for any length of time.

Watching movies, they need to 'take a break', same on journeys. If on the phone they have to walk/pace about, literally standing still in a queue they have to 'move about'. At first, seeing this it feels odd, then irritating, often you ask them to stop, to find they are unaware of their actions. Ultimately, it's something you learn to ignore and accept that they need to do this, it's not that they do it consciously as they want to, it's mainly sub-conscious and automatic. This I think is why part of the ADHD name says hyperactivity.

My approach: I point it out in good humour in situations where you would like it to stop and making them aware in a nice way helps that.

Mr Daydream

This sounds like a nice space to be in for anyone, 'away with the fairies' I have often said, a lovely expression I think, conjuring up images of floating in fantasy...This state happens very often for those with ADHD, they don't seem to be with you in the present moment.

Their mind has engaged them elsewhere with either an internal or external distraction and they get lost in their own thoughts for a while.

The 'while' is as short or long as a piece of string, I think this is where the other part of the ADHD name comes from – Attention Deficit.

My approach: I try hard to connect with him and bring him 'back into the room', as it were.

Mr Chatterbox

Speaks for itself this one, ha – see what I did there! No, don't worry, I won't give up my day job! When they are enthused and excited by something they will speak about it a lot and in my case very fast, so fast I had to slow him down to understand him. It's as if he can't get the words out quick enough, the energy is palpable.

This state in stark contrast to when he is the Dreamer and one of my favourites of his states, the energy is infectious.

My approach: I just enjoy the moment.

Mr Bump

Hmmm even the thought of this one fills me with anxiety (and I am not the anxious type!) again not sure this one needs much explanation, think of the expression 'bull in a china shop'. The speed at which he moves sometimes it's as if time is running out and the message is act fast...this is where things get spilt, broken or he literally stubs his toes or bashes his hands on surfaces or doors.

My approach: A gentle or not so gentle prompt of 'slow down' usually does the trick and snaps him back into normal speed instead of speed x 100.

Mr Cheerful

Unlike with the above state of being this one fills me with joy. His character is so likeable, it's not a stretch to say everyone likes him. This state comes and goes, I feel it happens when he has all his ducks in a row, not dissimilar to how most of us are I suppose but he is more affected by outside influences. He needs to not be tired, not hungry, not feeling under any pressure to do something e.g. from me or teachers, he needs to have plenty of time ahead of him.

It's when all these things happen simultaneously that he is at his best and relaxed.

My approach: I personally try very hard to ensure that as many things I can help control are done. I see myself as the person with the broom in front of the curling stone being sent down the ice, the smoother I make it, the more he glides...Of course I try to encourage him to sleep and eat, get on top of school work etc by himself but more often than not I have to play hard ball and make him do those things, not fun but the result ultimately is, as he becomes Mr Cheerful once more, so it is what it is and part of being there for someone with ADHD.

Mr Lazy

Controversial to say they are lazy, it's not as simple as that but it certainly 'appears' that they are. Without really knowing it, they are constantly weighing up every situation with – "well, what's in it for me". They seem to have an internal rewards-based system, they will do something if they gain something from it, otherwise what's the point. You could argue, that makes sense and we are all like that, yes and that could be true but in those with ADHD they aren't affected by some of society's norms. Examples could be seeing something as still clean for longer than most, seeing something as 'not that untidy', finding being a 'bit' late not really a big problem.

My approach: All I can say here is find a massive amount of patience, dig deep you are going to need it!

Mr Messy

As mentioned in the state Mr Lazy, being surrounded by mess and chaos seems to be invisible to them. Even when pointed out they say it's really not that bad. What that I think translates into is, it's not that important to them and they don't really care.

That to them is definitely 'sweating the small stuff' and in their mind unnecessary apart from a good sort from time to time – oh but they certainly don't ever mind you having a tidy up, just as long as you don't move anything, 'huh' I hear you say.

What they don't mind is, absolutely, find dirty clothes, plates, sheets and clean them by all means but do not put anything away in a drawer or cupboard, as they will never find it.

Most items need to be out, in their line of vision, to be accessible, otherwise 'out of sight, out of mind' plays a big part here.

My approach: I came up with places for things and always return them to those places, that seems to be working.

Mr Adventure

The more adventure the better for him, he would have it all the time if he could. That ticks all the boxes, gets his brain engaged and challenged. When something is exciting or exhilarating, he is at his best. He focuses and can keep concentrating for far longer than when he is another state.

My approach: I have always tried to seek out adrenaline-filed activities, this has ensured great entertainment and fun for all.

Mr Funny

He has a great sense of humour and I have noticed this often with those with ADHD, they have a sharp quick wit, maybe because their brain, when engaged has so many thoughts, so fast that they are the first to come up with a funny comment.

My approach: Just enjoy and belly laugh, it's an amazing natural tonic for all.

Mr Forgetful

My word, what can I say, he is unbelievably forgetful, I am mid menopause and have complete brain fog and although I now struggle with remembering some things, it's nothing in comparison to him. They have to act immediately on their thoughts/needs or they forget. Imagine walking downstairs and forgetting why, we all do that sometimes you say, well this is nearly every time. He forgets, where he needs to be, dates, times, deadlines...the list is endless.

It also extends to other important things though, he forgets to eat, shower, go to the toilet. The signals that tell him he is hungry, thirsty, I must dress, I need a shower are overpowered by whatever he is doing. He can be doing anything, climbing, playing games, be on his phone, watching TV, it is not until the situation becomes one of urgency does he respond...then he has to run to the toilet, eat immediately, anything that is to hand, he is unable to wait to cook or make something.

He realises he needs to be somewhere with minutes to go and rushes a shower and getting dressed.

My approach: A tough one but I suggest you need to act like his PA (Personal Assistant), sounds crazy I know but I has worked for me and him.

Mr Brave

Not much worries him or concerns him and he is a risk taker. In most cases this is useful and gives him confidence and allows him to do things some of us would not even think of, let alone try, this is the state I think produces entrepreneurs. When combined with their impulsivity it can lead to mistakes.

My approach: In an ideal world they have someone they can double check their decisions and ideas with before 'pressing the button'. Get them to open up about their thoughts, give them suggestions to think of as well. Usually, any advice is met with neutrality but after they have time to ponder, they often see your point of view and reasoning to perhaps change plans or just put on hold for a while.

Little Miss Late

Another that is self-explanatory. I have observed three distinct reasons for perpetual lateness in those with ADHD.

Firstly, they are engrossed and distracted and have not paid attention to the time.

Secondly, they have underestimated the time it takes to prepare or get there or carry out the task.

Thirdly, a very specific one for those with ADHD, they have either consciously or often unconsciously left it to the last minute to help with the motivation of getting ready, getting sorted, finishing the work. With the third reason they need the pressure that the threat of lateness creates to engage themselves but also to make it fun, they enjoy the challenge it presents them.

My approach: Shout at the top of your voice we are going to be late for the 1000th time – joking! Seriously the only one getting stressed is you, they simply don't care enough about lateness to stress about it and are often taken aback by how others are getting irritated. You need to employ tricks, they know and again don't care. You'd think they wouldn't work because they know but actually, they do work and then it's a win/win, you are happy and they are happy that you are not annoyed with them. The trick, tell them an earlier time, very simple but very effective.

Mr Angry

His anger doesn't happen often or is it aimed at people but when it happens it comes out of nowhere like it's travelled 0-60mph in a matter of seconds.

Most of the time it is provoked by gaming. Gaming is the only thing that he can get absorbed in and stay put for a while, I believe it's the adrenaline and constant need for interaction that works on multiple levels for him. But so engrossed he can get very frustrated with the game or himself, when it's not going well. This can cause him to shout or bang down his controller or headphones.

Moments later the anger has gone like it was never there in the first place. Anger also appears when things aren't going his way or as he expected, for example if he can't find something or if something is stuck, he would push or pull till it breaks.

My approach: I constantly try to encourage him to walk away from the game, take himself out of that environment, even if it's just for 5 minutes. Quite often if I can hear an outburst I walk in and tell him to stop, this usually snaps him out of the mode and stops it escalating. We are always working on ways he can prevent getting angry and best ways to deal with it when it does. Accepting the issue and addressing it is a big step and the anger outbursts are happening less and less frequently now.

Little Miss Inventor

He looks at any given situation with fresh eyes, kind of like 'Groundhog Day' if you know the film. Each day is a fresh new one with a blank canvas, so he is able to constantly add and update his ways of doing things. He doesn't just repeat what he did before.

A really good example of this is when he unloads the dishwasher (it's a rare event, don't get me started on how many reminders he needs).

Each time he puts the glasses and cups away he produces a different pattern and layout in the cupboard. Not like me who puts them where I always put them, I do the job without any thought whatsoever.

He on the other hand thinks and comes up what lots of interesting and ingenious ways to store them. This is the bit that makes them inventors, they don't follow anything or anyone, they think 'outside the box' as the saying goes, very often their way is an improvement or at the very least an interesting alternative.

My approach: Stand back and watch in awe.

Mr Generous

The expression 'generous to a fault' springs to mind here, oh and another 'money burns a whole in their pocket'.

Quite simply when they have money they spend until it's all gone.

They will spend on you or them, on treats, purchases anything really.

They would give you their last penny and often I have seen my son buying something for himself and for the homeless person outside the shop.

Their kindness is genuine and unconditional but back to the first statement, they don't think enough about the future and once whatever they are sharing is all gone, what then?

My approach: You need to make sure they put some money in savings or aside.

THINGS THOSE WITH ADHD MAY DO ON ANY GIVEN DAY...

- Calling someone and hoping they won't answer

- Boiling water for tea for the 7th time

- Regretting the plans that they made for after work

- Buying a new phone charger because they lost it again

- Wondering if they forgot to take their ADHD medication

- Working late because they didn't get anything done all day

- Finding one dirty spot in their home and doing a whole deep clean

- Losing track of what they were doing in the first place

BENEFITS TO HAVING ADHD

- Ability to hyperfocus
- Resilient
- Very creative and think 'outside the box'
- Engaging conversational skills
- Spontaneous
- Have abundant energy
- Great sense of humour
- Generous
- Empathetic
- A sense of fairness
- Willing to take a risk
- Romantic
- Persistent
- Compassionate

THE NEED TO MANAGE ADHD AND HOW

When ADHD is NOT managed, it can lead to anxiety, depression and other health problems.

- Having ADHD can be tiring and frustrating for those with ADHD but also for those around those with ADHD – parents, partners, colleagues etc.
- Understanding what is happening and why is beneficial for all.
- Having ADHD is like having a race car brain with bicycle breaks.
- ADHD can be seen as a superpower when something is challenging and matters to you. Niagara Falls could just be seen as a lot of mist and noise when up close but harness its power and it can light up New York.
- Those with ADHD can live a better life with less effort when their ADHD is managed well.

The best way to manage is with plenty of exercise, good sleep, good nutrition and any stress reduction plus any of the below list:

- Practice Mindfulness - e.g. take a walk and try listening out for birds, the concentration will help with a busy mind
- Work to your strengths – save the battle with things that you find difficult
- Break tasks in to chunks - work in a pattern of short bursts, followed by short breaks

- To take a break try the 5, 4, 3, 2, 1 game – the 5 senses. 5 things you can hear, 4 things you see, 3 things you can touch, 2 things you can taste, 1 thing you can smell
- Stand when possible whilst working - this will allow the body to constantly move as is so often needed by those with ADHD
- Have a pen and paper by your bed - to note down anything that may be on your mind that is stopping you sleep or record on your phone
- Use your phone as a helpful devise - for reminders, lists and as a recording device
- Show yourself your schedule visually – this can be better sometimes
- Connect with a person, an animal or nature - this will really help with wellbeing.

MY PARTING WORDS...

To encapsulate ADHD, this is the response from my son when I asked him would he like to read my first draft, a book that is predominately about him, "Not really, that's long"

I laughed so much. His use of the word long is not about the length of the book, he has no idea how long it is, it is slang for something that is difficult or annoying or not worth the effort!

He and I talked often as I wrote the book and he is completely aware of the sort of things in it, so for him, nothing is new or novel or interesting – it is about him so he knows that stuff already!

I personally have enjoyed going back over the last 16 years remembering some of the moments, there are of course, so many more but I tried to include the ones that could be relatable and show ADHD at its finest.

It was great to see how far we have come in building our AWARENESS, UNDERSTANDING and ACCEPTANCE.

QUOTE – ALBERT EINSTEIN

If you judge
a fish by its
ability to climb a tree,
it will live its
whole life believing
it is stupid

APPPENDIX 1

SUGGESTIONS ON HOW TO HELP THOSE WITH ADHD INCLUDING WHILST AT WORK

Administrative Tasks – these can be a struggle for a variety of reasons, including that they are often viewed as dull and repetitive. Any support will help, even if it is just reminders.

Written Information – any information given verbally can be mis-heard, mis-understood or simply forgotten. Having things noted down or backed up with a message or email helps eliminate some of the issues.

SMART Goals - any goals/work to be agreed collaboratively, any questions can be asked and expectations made clear.

Good Communication – regular check-ins and effective communication will ensure that there is less room for overthinking or ruminating. It will also reassure someone who is finding it difficult to ask.

Distractions – some find it most helpful to use noise cancelling headphones, not only do they block out outside noise they also go some way to block out the constant 'noise' from their mind if they listen to music, this in turn helps them focus better.

Memory – some find it useful to have prompts and reminders sent close to plans, meetings and deadlines, also including the documentation or links to, in order to prepare in advance.

Trust – extend them the trust that they know when they need a break or to work from home or a quiet space and allow them to feel understood and supported.

Time Keeping – this can be quite a struggle for some, ask them how you can help, it may be that you encourage them to adopt a process of setting artificial meeting start times and deadlines and they are ready before the actual time needed.

Motivation – watch for hyperfocus moments of intense work (for something they find interesting and novel), a period of burnout can often follow. Help them regulate and get started on tasks that don't hold much interest for them.

Ideas – give them opportunity to use their energy and creativity with having regular meetings to discuss things openly.

Printed in Great Britain
by Amazon